10
SELF-EXPLORATION

A SELF-DISCOVERY JOURNAL

Questions And Prompts That Will Help You Gain
Self-Awareness In Less Than 10 Minutes A Day

BY AMY J. BLAKE

INTRODUCTION

Hey there,

My name is Amy and I will guide YOU through your 100 day journaling challenge of self-discovery.

It is well established by now and if you picked up this book you probably already know this, journaling as a habit comes along with a multitude of benefits.

Benefits such as:

- Increasing self-confidence
- Sparking creativity
- Strengthening self-discipline
- Evoking mindfulness
- Expanding IQ
- ...
- But more importantly — **self-discovery**

And that"s the sole purpose of this journal!
To be a guide that will enable you to re-discover yourself and help

you become self-aware (*while spending less than 10 minutes a day*).

So I challenge YOU to start your journey of self-exploration TODAY and commit to journal on a daily basis for the next 100 days!

Once finished, you will be amazed by the results; you will have picked up a healthy and productive daily habit and will have experienced the benefits of journaling first hand.

So what are you still waiting for, let"s get right to it!

Cheers,
Amy Blake

DAY: 1

DATE:.................................

WHO ARE YOU?

....

....

....

....

....

....

....

....

....

DATE:......................................

WHAT ARE YOU PASSIONATE ABOUT?

....

....

....

....

....

....

....

....

....

DAY: 3

DATE:.............................

WHAT ARE YOU MOST <u>FOR</u> <u>GRATEFUL IN LIFE?</u>

....

....

....

....

....

....

....

....

....

DAY: 4

DATE:................................

WHAT ARE YOUR VALUES?

....

....

....

....

....

....

....

....

....

DAY: 5

DATE:...............................

WHAT ARE THE 3 BIGGEST THINGS YOU'VE LEARNED IN LIFE TO DATE?

....

....

....

....

....

....

....

....

....

DAY: 6

DATE:............................

WHAT ADVICE WOULD YOU GIVE TO YOURSELF 3 YEARS AGO?

....

....

....

....

....

....

....

....

DATE:.....................................

WHAT DO YOU FEAR? HOW CAN YOU OVERCOME IT?

....

....

....

....

....

....

....

....

....

DATE:..................................

WHAT ARE YOU WORRIED ABOUT? WILL IT MATTER 3 YEARS FROM NOW?

....

....

....

....

....

....

....

....

....

DATE:................................

WHAT ARE YOUR BIGGEST GOALS AND DREAMS?

....

....

....

....

....

....

....

....

....

DATE:.................................

IF YOU COULD DO SOMETHING FOR FREE FOR THE REST OF YOUR LIFE, WHAT WOULD IT BE?

....

....

....

....

....

....

....

....

DATE:...............................

WHAT WOULD YOU DO IF YOU KNEW YOU COULD NOT FAIL & THERE WERE NO LIMITATION OF RESOURCES (MONEY, TIME, ...) ?

....

....

....

....

....

....

....

....

DAY: 12

DATE:.................................

WHAT'S STOPPING YOU NOW & HOW CAN YOU OVERCOME IT?

....

....

....

....

....

....

....

....

....

DATE:................................

ARE YOU PUTTING ANY PARTS OF YOUR LIFE ON HOLD? (HONESTLY)

....

....

....

....

....

....

....

....

DAY: 14

DATE:...................................

WHAT'S THE TOP PRIORITY IN YOUR LIFE RIGHT NOW?

....

....

....

....

....

....

....

....

100 DAYS OF SELF DISCOVERY

DATE:....................................

WHAT AND WHO MAKES YOU HAPPY?

....

....

....

....

....

....

....

....

....

DATE:................................

WHAT IS SOMETHING YOU REGRET DOING? IS IT AFFECTING YOU TO THIS DAY?

....

....

....

....

....

....

....

....

....

DATE:.................................

WHAT IS A POSITIVE MEMORY THAT STANDS OUT FROM YOUR CHILDHOOD?

....

....

....

....

....

....

....

....

DATE:............................

WHAT IS A NEGATIVE MEMORY THAT STANDS OUT FROM YOUR CHILDHOOD? WHAT DID YOU LEARN FROM IT?

....

....

....

....

....

....

....

....

DATE:...............................

WHAT LIMITING BELIEFS ARE YOU HOLDING ON TO?

....

....

....

....

....

....

....

....

....

DATE:.................................

WHAT EMPOWERING BELIEFS CAN YOU TAKE ON MOVING FORWARD?

....

....

....

....

....

....

....

....

....

DATE:...........................

WHAT ARE SOME BAD HABITS YOU WANT TO REPLACE?

....

....

....

....

....

....

....

....

DATE:...................................

WHAT GOOD HABITS YOU WANT TO CULTIVATE INSTEAD?

....

....

....

....

....

....

....

....

DATE:..................................

WHERE ARE YOU LIVING RIGHT NOW?
PAST, FUTURE OR PRESENT?

....

....

....

....

....

....

....

....

DATE:....................................

WHAT IS YOUR LIFE'S PURPOSE? WHAT IS YOUR MISSION?

....

....

....

....

....

....

....

....

....

DATE:................................

WHAT DRIVES YOU? WHY DO YOU WAKE UP EVERY DAY?

....

....

....

....

....

....

....

....

DAY: 26

DATE:...................................

HOW CAN YOU MAKE YOUR LIFE MORE MEANINGFUL STARTING TODAY?

....

....

....

....

....

....

....

....

....

DATE:.................................

HOW CAN YOU CHANGE SOMEONE'S LIFE FOR THE BETTER TODAY?

....

....

....

....

....

....

....

....

DATE:...................................

WHO ARE THE 5 PEOPLE YOU SPEND THE MOST TIME WITH?

....

....

....

....

....

....

....

....

DATE:..................................

ARE THESE PEOPLE HOLDING YOU BACK OR PUSHING YOU FORWARD?

....

....

....

....

....

....

....

....

DATE:....................................

WHAT IS YOUR IDEAL LIFE PARTNER LIKE?

....

....

....

....

....

....

....

....

....

DAY: 31

DATE:...................................

ARE YOU AFRAID OF LETTING OTHERS GET CLOSE TO YOU? IF SO, WHY?

....

....

....

....

....

....

....

....

DATE:...................................

WHO IS THE MOST IMPORTANT PERSON TO YOU IN THE WORLD?

....

....

....

....

....

....

....

....

....

DATE:...................................

HAVE YOU LET HIM/HER KNOW HOW MUCH YOU VALUE THEIR CONTRIBUTIONS TO YOUR LIFE?

....

....

....

....

....

....

....

....

DATE:....................................

WHAT IS YOUR IDEAL CAREER?

....

....

....

....

....

....

....

....

....

DATE:...................................

HOW CAN YOU START CREATING YOUR IDEAL CAREER STARTING TODAY?

....

....

....

....

....

....

....

....

DATE:...............................

WHAT IS YOUR IDEAL DIET?

....

....

....

....

....

....

....

....

....

....

DATE:..

WHAT DO YOU NEED TO DO TO ACHIEVE YOUR IDEAL DIET?

....

....

....

....

....

....

....

....

DATE:..................................

WHAT IS YOUR IDEAL HOME LIKE?

....

....

....

....

....

....

....

....

....

DATE:................................

WHAT DO YOU NEED TO DO TO ACHIEVE YOUR IDEAL HOME?

....

....

....

....

....

....

....

....

DATE:...................................

<u>WHAT IS YOUR IDEAL PHYSICAL LOOK?</u>

....

....

....

....

....

....

....

....

....

DATE:................................

WHAT DO YOU NEED TO DO TO ACHIEVE YOUR IDEAL PHYSICAL LOOK?

....

....

....

....

....

....

....

....

....

DATE:................................

WHAT IS YOUR IDEAL LIFE?

DATE:..............................

WHAT CAN YOU DO TODAY TO START LIVING YOUR IDEAL LIFE?

....

....

....

....

....

....

....

....

DATE:...................................

WHAT WOULD YOU WANT TO SAY TO YOURSELF 3 YEARS IN THE FUTURE?

....

....

....

....

....

....

....

....

DATE:...............................

IS THERE ANYTHING YOU ARE RUNNING AWAY FROM?

....

....

....

....

....

....

....

....

....

DATE:..

ARE YOU SETTLING FOR LESS THAN WHAT YOU ARE WORTH? WHY?

....

....

....

....

....

....

....

....

DATE:....................................

IF YOU ONLY HAD 1 YEAR TO LIVE, HOW WOULD YOU SPEND IT?

....

....

....

....

....

....

....

....

WHAT IS SOMETHING YOU WANT TO DO BUT HAVE NOT DONE TO DATE?

....

....

....

....

....

....

....

....

DATE:................................

IF YOU HAD MILLIONS OF DOLLARS, HOW WOULD YOU SPEND IT?

....

....

....

....

....

....

....

....

DATE:..

ARE YOU A GIVER OR A TAKER?

DATE:............................

WHERE/HOW WOULD YOU LIKE TO SEE YOURSELF IN 10 YEARS FROM NOW?

....

....

....

....

....

....

....

....

DATE:..................................

ARE YOU OPEN-MINDED? JUDGEMENTAL?

....

....

....

....

....

....

....

....

....

DAY: 53

DATE:..

WHAT WOULD YOU LIKE TO CHANGE ABOUT YOURSELF?

....

....

....

....

....

....

....

....

DATE:.....................................

WHAT DO YOU LIKE ABOUT YOURSELF?

DATE:...................................

IF YOU HAD TO DESCRIBE YOURSELF USING 10 WORDS, WHAT WOULD THOSE BE?

....

....

....

....

....

....

....

....

DAY: 56

DATE:................................

IF YOU COULD TALK TO YOUR TEENAGE SELF, WHAT WOULD YOU SAY?

....

....

....

....

....

....

....

....

DATE:..

WHAT SURPRISED YOU THE MOST ABOUT YOUR LIFE OR LIFE IN GENERAL?

....

....

....

....

....

....

....

....

DATE:.................................

WHAT CAN YOU LEARN FROM YOUR BIGGEST MISTAKE TO DATE?

....

....

....

....

....

....

....

....

....

DATE:..............................

WHAT'S A TOPIC YOU NEED TO LEARN MORE ABOUT TO HELP YOU LIVE A MORE FULFILLING LIFE?

....

....

....

....

....

....

....

....

DATE:.................................

WRITE 10 THINGS YOU WOULD LIKE TO SAY NO TO:

....

....

....

....

....

....

....

....

....

....

DATE:................................

WRITE 10 THINGS YOU WOULD LIKE TO SAY YES TO:

....

....

....

....

....

....

....

....

....

....

DAY: 62

DATE:.................................

WHEN DO YOU FEEL HAPPIEST THE MOST?

....

....

....

....

....

....

....

....

....

DATE:..

<u>WHEN DO YOU FEEL ENERGIZED THE MOST?</u>

....

....

....

....

....

....

....

....

....

DATE:.................................

WRITE ONE THING YOU WISH OTHERS KNEW ABOUT YOU:

....

....

....

....

....

....

....

....

DATE:...................................

WHAT WOULD BE CONSIDERED ENOUGH FOR YOU?

....

....

....

....

....

....

....

....

....

DATE:.................................

WHAT COULD YOU NOT IMAGINE LIVING WITHOUT?

....

....

....

....

....

....

....

....

....

DATE:...................................

WHAT IS YOUR FAVORITE WAY OF SPENDING THE DAY?

....

....

....

....

....

....

....

....

DATE:.................................

<u>WRITE 10 THINGS THAT MAKE YOU SMILE:</u>

....

....

....

....

....

....

....

....

....

DAY: 69

DATE:...................................

WRITE 10 WORDS YOU WOULD LIKE TO LIVE BY:

....

....

....

....

....

....

....

....

....

DATE:.................................

IF TODAY WAS YOUR LAST DAY EVER, WHO WOULD YOU WANT TO SPEND IT WITH?

....

....

....

....

....

....

....

....

DATE:...............................

WHAT ARE YOU TRULY GRATEFUL FOR? DO YOU EXPRESS YOUR THANKFULNESS?

DATE:...................................

<u>DO YOU ENJOY LIFE? HOW CAN YOU EXPERIENCE</u>
<u>MORE ENJOYMENT?</u>

....

....

....

....

....

....

....

....

DAY: 73

DATE:.................................

<u>DO YOU SEE YOURSELF AS SUCCESSFUL?</u>

....

....

....

....

....

....

....

....

....

DAY: 74

DATE:..............................

WHAT ARE YOU PROUD OF HAVING ACHIEVED?

....

....

....

....

....

....

....

....

....

DATE:......................................

WHAT IS SOMETHING YOU ARE ASHAMED OF? HOW CAN YOU DEAL WITH THIS?

....

....

....

....

....

....

....

....

DATE:.................................

WHAT DO YOU NEED RIGHT NOW MORE THAN ANYTHING ELSE?

....

....

....

....

....

....

....

....

DATE:..............................

WHAT ARE YOU RESISTING, OR ATTACHING TO?

....

....

....

....

....

....

....

....

....

....

DATE:...................................

WHAT ARE YOUR GIFTS? HOW CAN YOU SHARE THEM WITH THE WORLD?

....

....

....

....

....

....

....

....

DATE:...............................

WHAT IS THE THING YOU ARE SECOND MOST PROUD OF?

....

....

....

....

....

....

....

....

DATE:...................................

WHAT KIND OF LEGACY DO YOU WANT TO LEAVE BEHIND?

....

....

....

....

....

....

....

....

DAY: 81

DATE:................................

HOW DO YOU FEEL ABOUT YOUR PARENTS?

....

....

....

....

....

....

....

....

....

DATE:...................................

HOW IS YOUR RELATIONSHIP WITH MONEY?

....

....

....

....

....

....

....

....

....

....

DATE:................................

WHAT ARE YOUR BIGGEST FEARS ABOUT SUCCESS?

....

....

....

....

....

....

....

....

....

DAY: 84

DATE:................................

WHAT MOTIVATES YOU THE MOST?

....

....

....

....

....

....

....

....

....

DATE:..

WHO IS YOUR GREATEST ROLE MODEL?

....

....

....

....

....

....

....

....

....

DATE:...................................

WHAT IS SOMETHING THAT IS TRUE FOR YOU NO MATTER WHAT?

....

....

....

....

....

....

....

....

DATE:..

WHAT IS YOUR MORAL COMPASS IN MAKING TOUGH DECISIONS?

....

....

....

....

....

....

....

....

....

DAY: 88

DATE:....................................

WHAT IS YOUR HIGHEST CORE VALUE?

....

....

....

....

....

....

....

....

....

DATE:..............................

WHAT DO YOU BELIEVE IS POSSIBLE FOR YOU?

....

....

....

....

....

....

....

....

....

DATE:.....................................

IF YOU COULD HAVE ONE SINGLE WISH GRANTED, WHAT WOULD IT BE?

....

....

....

....

....

....

....

....

DATE:....................................

IF YOU COULD START OVER, WHO WOULD YOU BE?

....

....

....

....

....

....

....

....

DAY: 92

DATE:.................................

WHAT IS THE ONE REGRET YOU DO NOT WANT TO HAVE IN YOUR LIFETIME?

....

....

....

....

....

....

....

....

DATE:...................................

WHAT DO YOU LIKE THE MOST AND LEAST ABOUT YOUR DAILY LIFE?

....

....

....

....

....

....

....

....

DATE:...............................

IS YOUR LIFE MOVING TOWARDS A POSITIVE OR NEGATIVE DIRECTION? WHY?

....

....

....

....

....

....

....

....

DATE:..............................

WHAT ARE THE 3 MOST IMPORTANT THINGS YOU HAVE LEARNED ABOUT YOURSELF?

....

....

....

....

....

....

....

....

DAY: 96

DATE:................................

WHAT VISION DO YOU HAVE FOR YOUR LIFE MOVING FORWARD?

....

....

....

....

....

....

....

....

DAY: 97

DATE: ....

<u>WHAT DO YOU LOVE ABOUT TODAY?</u>

....

....

....

....

....

....

....

....

....

DAY: 98

DATE:....................................

WHAT ARE YOU MOST GRATEFUL FOR TODAY?

....

....

....

....

....

....

....

....

....

DAY: 99

DATE:................................

<u>AGAIN...WHO ARE YOU?</u>

....

....

....

....

....

....

....

....

....

DAY: 100

DATE:..............................

<u>WHAT ARE GOING TO DO DIFFRENTLY AFTER COMPLETING THIS CHALLENGE?</u>

....

....

....

....

....

....

....

....

CONGRATULATIONS

You made it to the very end! Give yourself a hearty pat on the back, you certainly deserve it!

I know this was only a journal but don't let that diminish its value in any way. YOU devoted more than three months of your life to this and hopefully now you have reached the end, you have a better understanding of your priorities, values and dreams moving forward!

Being self-aware is probably the single most important skill anyone can learn, because only then you can clearly and objectively evaluate your strengths and weaknesses. Once you do so you can make the most of them in any situation regardless of the circumstances at play.

That being said, I wish you the very best moving forward and would love to hear if and how this journal helped you in any way!

To Your Success,
Amy Blake

Made in the USA
San Bernardino, CA
10 April 2017